Take It In

Cover Photo: Ahu Smith
Cover Design: Shine Borovi

Rustled Paper Publishing
I.S.B.N. 978-91-639-4661-5

This is dedicated to the one that got away.

"The dream was always running ahead of me. To catch up, to live for a moment in unison with it, that was the miracle."

— Anais Nin

Introduction

I allow lights entrance, letting my body ooze with emotional movement. It's in the willingness to confront myself. In that moment. Allow the doing or saying to arrive within me through innocence. Know nothing and feel everything. Naiveté keeps my heart young, curiosity strong. I use to think naiveté was a weakness. Now I know it's why I can love, fully, over and over again. It's because in that moment I've never loved before, never done this before, I've never seen this before. Being in the not knowing the knowing of everything enters.

Allow your senses total charge.

Feel heart pulse through your entire body.

Believe in love.

Breathe that in and feel the touch of every single solitary You.

Love Poem to the Air

Soft calico breeze brushes my face,
going under, lifting my pure white gandora.
Walking feels of warm velvet,
slow cascade around loose hips.
You follow me all day, lifting me up,
beyond my fantasy of wanting.
Nightfall brings deeper heart caressing,
song angels, a lover all in heart.
The air. The air. Breathe me in.
You are all I desire.

Blue City

Caressing. Whispers. Elevated life.
Strident through blue blue in all colors I walk.
Gaze penetrates this sensuous sumptuous soul.
Untamed pause, a cause.

Water hears me. I pass.
Birds fly low. I lie down.
Tall grass, red poppy. Rolling tumble.
Voluptuous moss.

I turn, lay heart and heat with coffee and cream
velvet skin. Perfect human love entanglement.
Yes in his smile. Deep open moans.
Salty tears.

Exotic flavors of mystical mythical magic.
Lifetimes. Daytime.
Night breeze.
Chocolate kisses whispered.

To say, Yes,
I will love from a loving, trusting, sharing, beating heart,
my most important being doing.

flow

cold metal flow
bubbles round
fingers lowered on woman
searching for
the same flow that comes
between our eyes
I need you to touch my flow
wake up

SouLFirE

Quiver and Shake through rolling hills.
I'm new born of red and gold.
My light blinding.
My body new and old.
Quiver and Shake.
Inside a volcano erupts.
I fly across large green hills, green bushes.
What's this?
I'm stilted in sky.
Quiver and Shake.
Red gold blue snow covers these hills.
Sand covers these hills.
Rain covers these hills.
Water moves.
Earthquake.
Quiver and Shake.
Reckless flying.
Blinded by beauty.
Blinded by my own bright light.
Walls of white pour out of my crying heart,
flowing me part of everything.
Crowds of people look up, see beauty flying.
Where are you?
Do you love alone?
Quiver and Shake.
Are you alone?
Quiver and Shake
I roam and roam.

The sands of the Sahara, blown in my face,
carry no annoyance. I am home to my sand filled lungs.
Dry hot desert sand, camel rides, and chosen stars,
carry light to my sand filled bed.
Sexing them, I feel the grit cut my skin.
My pleasure, my heart.
My soul embraced in safety, love and deep longing
celebrate alienation along dunes of eternity.
Nips of insight graze by. I catch them.
I breathe in the smell of this funky, dirty, stinky
Moroccan homage of dream filled architecture,
call to prayer and dark eyed men with
passions aggressively peaceful.
Buried and healed I am lifted so high I
orgasm in relief of all places,
ever will be, can be, am be.
The arms of universal lifetimes
carry me home.

Bruise stained forgiveness crawls over these tall dunes. Wind
blows knowing of love received and given. Passionate anger and
frustration the ink upon my skin, scars deep. Oblivion lives in
Mama's eyes, sister's repudiation, brother's compromise.
I am chosen from the gatherers of warrior courage.
Genetics absolved. Dimensions separate us. Love, our tax.

Daddy Said....

That's my girl.

Beans beans for your heart, the more you eat the more you like 'em.

I know I lived before as an East Indian man. I could wrap a Turban around my head better than them.

Be in the basement when I come home.

This doesn't work anymore does it, well, I'm gonna find something that does.

You got your rhythm from me.

I can't give you anymore, I'm sorry.

Don't touch me.

What did you do to your hair?

You always need a black dress.

Never let him go.

Ten up, ten down.

Your Mama had this idea that she was pregnant.

He ate 'er!

He's left handed.

All politicians are crooks.

I hate hypocrites.

You don't know what you want. If you did, you wouldn't be here.

What do you want to know now? ... when I'm gonna die?

I'm coming back one more time.

That's right. That's it.

I've never met a stranger.

The past is not important.

Work now, play later.

See that Nigger over there? He'll cut off your ears.

I don't care if he's sittin' on my shoulders.

Love you, Squirt.

Terri, Terri, Terri, Terri

Go ahead, call the cops. When they get here, I'll shoot 'em.

Yeah I'm crazy because that's how I'm suppose to be.
Sit back, relax. Breathe the crazy, sit up with crazy,
roll shoulders with crazy, feel the pain of crazy.
Let the baby be the baby. Kick and scream, throw glass bottles.
You know, the axe computers in half kinda crazy.
You will feel the edge of your eyes, ears, nose, mouth, knees.
Shall I go on?
Keep listening for mirrors living inside you, cats, deers.
Close your eyes. Hear those cats constantly meow screaming.
Get up. See how you will help.

Girl, Girl, Girl. Am I a girl? Am I a boy?
Wait, I like girl. Girl twisted heart. Girl twisted heat. Girl all over me.
Closets, bushes, stripped naked window to window, kissing, bondage,
escape into girlhood. Boys? yuck--pulling, tugging, breathing heavy
in my ears. What Am I?

Christian South punishment, hard times in a room alone with no
food, no trust, no water, no place to crawl to. Okay, I'll tear my
paper, claw my clothes, play match box cars and make my dolls
fuck each other.

Truth? Doesn't happen here in the South. Trust? That neither.
Especially for a wild child with wetness of girl between her legs.
Okay, let's outside, lets hide. Cuz tomorrow, black and blue welts
on my backside.

I won't sit still for Mama and Daddy. Only for the girl.
Girls. Girls. Girls. Break em' open and see what's inside.
Luscious fruit, sweet tangy messy slimy fruit plucked from southern
suburban trees. Creeks pour out snakes we run from. Hiding,
spying, looking into the forest for truth we can't find in our wooden
pink and white homes.

Firebird Return_____

A slipping sliding dance for ages.
Sliding into the hope of a shift.
Thinking during a heart song.
Reggae thumps and I feel nothing of what I showed before.
The Bird Family I've always said, always will say, until
I die a natural sudden death.
Resurrection a kill handled by unknown Kings and Queens in quicksand.
Melted glass with holes and ridges.
Sand paper speech talks to the Swallow.
A small bird. Gentle, shy with soft feathers, the bountied sweet call.
A tweet, a palm sweaty and who cares.
Hot insights of something I won't show outside.
He laughed once I became real and stole the show.
The intimate entertainer.
Either I'm buried in ash or I've risen.
Which one?

I'm broken down Albino Injun' from Bird Tribe,
purple blue wings hidden from plain view.
I chase Lizard for food,
feasting on green brown crunchy tail.
I run from village to village,
in white hot dried Desert,
seducing arms to hold me on earth.
I cover from neck to tail.
My fleshy arms sag with distant memory of present moments.
I remember nothing except the hunt for belonging love.
Some days I look up to Golden Sun and see myself flying,
swooping, soaring, wings outspread,
my purple turned red and my blues to white light.
Stumbling through sweet sage brush,
cleansed with sweetest nectar, I fall, pierced.
In my falling I rise. How high, this time?
I release my wings in balance,
carrying me up
through soft airs
into the
mouth
of
my
mother.

Love speaks up.

Love is marriage to yourself first.

Love is rhythm.

Love is a condition that makes itself known.

Love learns love.

Desert Voices

Squeezing jam juice through your hands told me let Life flow.
Realization through feeling action allows confrontation its space.
Spitting your laugh, saying "Pee Maw!."
Baby voice beginnings.
You lived alone, wrote on beautiful writing desk.
Pen in your beautiful hand. Mine like yours.
Birds singing on your high porch.
Dirt basement smells like home.
You showed me freedom.
Bus rides, watching Hippies.
Coca Cola every morning.
Ice water when you rest your head.
No shower at moon time.
Scarf adornment.
Keep your shoulders covered. Especially during sleep.
The big black rotary phone in the hall, two bedrooms made your home.
You told me Mama and Daddy really loved me.
Now you whisper in my ear.

The time has come to come undone.

The First

After the first stop I didn't see him in the van.
Where is he? I keep looking back over the hordes of
sweaty Berbers crammed in this vehicle.
Did he get out and not say goodbye?
M. said he was coming back with me.
Was he traded for another?
We stop again and again and still no sign of him.
I feel myself missing him.
Why didn't he say goodbye?
The next stop I get out,
letting the woman sitting next to me out.
There he is. He's been riding on top of the van.
Across the open Sahara.
He keeps his gaze on me as he unloads the goods.
Those eyes and how he looks at me...
he gets down and says, "Much better on top,
...the people's smells are too much for me. Skank."
More people get out making room for a few.
He gets in first, beckoning me with his eyes.
I slide in beside him.
Close.
The orange van sways toward destinations
delivering goods for Auberges and tiny Desert stores.
He places his body tight to mine.
His hand rests gentle and firm on the top of my left thigh.
I nestle my arm in his elbow space.
Feel held, safe. Feel belonging.
His knee shorter than mine, I slide my buttocks snug to the
back of the seat. Mine still longer.
His body small. His hands expressive and energetic.
I ask him about the ring on his finger.
Obsidian? Garnet?
"Take it off" I say.
"Okay, you try" he says laughing.
I do. It's snug and tight.
His hands, beauty. His face royal, chiseled, strong and commanding.
When I mention the beautiful woman in the front seat
he says "this is not the important thing.
It's the connection, do you agree?"
I say, "yes."
His presence and willingness doesn't push.
I may never see this man again.
I may only have this moment.

The Gift

Sand covers me. Wind storm causes chaos and memory loss.
I live right now, here, in my sandy skin. Sleep grinding me.
Beat constant from the E-Trance Festival Dance. You will find me
close by my man, protected from the storms. Storms of invitations,
roaming fingers and derelict blood.

My new Berber scarf contains history, young and old.
Mothers shouldered gift given for the first time.
Special richness covers our ritual hands.
Tears fall on the offering, christening the love.
Honored belonging holds me here, captures my past, washes the grief.
Sends me into his arms for my resolve. I am home. At last.

Mostly I just listen to the voices in my head that don't speak.

There are no stars tonight except within me.
Finally see the sparkles of light my life holds.
I smile tonight knowing of my journeys here and there.
Of my exotic, wonder full life.

Tonight there are no stars except within my perception.
I perceive abundance follows me, courts me, pleasures me.
I hold the key for my life treasure.
I hold the key of freedoms stability and loves song.

My heart opens for stars sparkling bright.
Those tiny points of light where I see through and know that
life stands in front of me, grasped lightly,
holding fast and loving long kindness everywhere.

Tonight star vision appeals to me,
abundance appeals to me,
love appeals to me.
Silent confidence covers my star blanket.

Always follow your breath.

This gives your guts a place for living.

The shoe fit in the desert. I longed to see him there. As he was. Then. I see only sorrow with laughter after the uhnn. The sound made when a slip occurs. A slice of darkness through the light. Obsessing, a game I've played a lifetime and now again here in this Blue City. He sits apart from me. I look at him incessantly. Watching for a sign that he doesn't love me anymore. His face stoic. My hunger unbearable. Always wanting more. Awake with the pain of a longing met in a desert.

Merzouga Dar

My hands go to my eyes.
I rub them in contemplation of my
present situation.
We all want to know exactly
what that is, yet we
forget that a gentle message
awaits us on the breeze,
calling us as we scratch
                our heads, roll our
shoulders, cry, laugh, joy.
When we sink in our holes
we can't seem to find the inspiration
        to go on.
We drink our tea, smoke our smoke
    and wonder when that message
will come.
    Along our path we stumble and
    where is the slice of light
        to enter?
    Sometimes secure in our fall,
    and mostly fallen, we
        reject the fall.
    Just standing up, walking to
        the next room a chore.

Take my eyes out of me
    because when I keep them in
I can't see.
    The knowing secluded in the
        unknowing.
The sadness succumbs to
    the past where the
joy awaits our attention.

Accept sadness as joy.
The river lets loose and
cleanses its path.
When I look back at
the raging river
I forget how the rain
started. It's gone.

The nights when hunger burns me, I accept it cold.
The days when the longly follows me, down there runs hot.
You'd think by now I'd die, I think so highly of myself.
You're wrong. My highs from highly, highly doubtful.
You'd think by now I'd fly. With feet firm planted on ground.

I have one little girl inside me. Avoidance.
Right now the story must be told.
The Greatest Story Ever Told pushes my boundaries.
Claws at my face. Strips melanin off my skin.
The worst kind of prejudice is against your own people.
Why retread what you right and backtrack to what's wrong?
Call me firebird. Call me the fucking Flame.

Our song played

I had nothing to do with it.
The rhythm lingered,
floating close to the surface
by those memory glands,
yet,
I had nothing to do
for it.
Awakened hope lies
deep down
churns the smoldering
constant pulse.
Brings forth
a calling only
known when I'm
through doors
of pain and loving residue.

Forgetting seems
impossible.
Regretting seems
distant.
Memories ooze
through the buds
of my coffee
stained tongue.

Consolation

My willingness to live becomes more transparent.
I must find a way back. A forward moving back.
I must not become the sadness.
I mustn't allow the cold rain to penetrate my resolve.
I must live the life my inner landscape demands.

There is a window. There is a rug.
There is a child. There is a kitchen table and chairs.
There is food. There is warmth. There is a bed to lay my head.
There is love. Everything works. I feel strong and healthy.
There is a chair. There is a towel hanging on the door.
There are dishes in the sink.

Stairs, up and down around this way, up and down that way. Across my face Axe cologne, nail polish, giggly girls and stoic faces. Moving, always moving. My back aches from moving and walking, stressing for the next train. Time a routine, business twenty four seven. I walk alone in these streets, up and down stairs and escalators. Elevators moving people for city meets and disco treats. Oh god I wish I drank the drink. Swallow that Fishermans lozenge for the one hundredth time to feel freshness somewhere. Up and down these city stairs meeting trains going out to quiet places for resting our heads and lying in our beds for another walk up and down the city stairs.

Contemplate a soulful place where rest beats your feet in the walk. Where do you lay your homelessness? The lull in the action from a long day beating the path toward nowhere in particular searching for the lost and found, the sheep and horse, the dragons breath, a familiar face watching into yours the same longing for a belonging among the humans stalking this place on Earth where beavers build dams in silence and the whispers howl in Swedish.

My battery low, my energy aching and slow, my mouth dry from lack of pure water from a bottle without bubbles. I am wound up. My face sqwenched like a wench in search of heart. What's funny? You with the blonde hair, perfect skin and bone structure. You with the calm fear of being found after your lost steps have drowned.

After the heart washed over my body, change rattled my soul.
I hear a call. A pulse with feminine blood. Softness becomes me.
Laughter, smiling eyes. Berber singing stays within this brain
landscape. Takes me back for swinging hips and open arms.
Dark eyes see me for the first time. I want to write about
something that has no words. My heart carries the longing
belonging through rubbish and the poverty of crippled religion.
I feel the sand of the Sahara holding me, calling me back.
And yet, here I am, in the cold bowels of Scandinavia.

sadness hangin' from my shoulders
drippy chocolate desirin' to be et
I wonder where my time is
my hair goes
my clothes on
clothes tossed
I feel like a deadhead redhead
I accept you for what you are
why can't I fix my leaky faucet
why can't I see up
when you got all the luck
are you gonna fuck
me
tuck
me
in at night
say you love
me
hold my ice cream cone
as it melts?

These Words She Spoke

She spoke about love
and how she misses it.
She spoke about loss
and how she regrets it.
She spoke about longing
and how she knows it.
She spoke about her life
and how she lives it.

She looked deep into
my eyes, her censors digging,
disturbing my equilibrium.
She spoke, "I long for
the loss of love."
"Please," she said,
"be fearless in love
because the loss of it is
the most beautiful thing.
The pain tells you."

Take It In

I lean, breathless against the Medina wall. My pulse quickened from the encounter. He is tall, dark and handsome. A Moroccan man with smoldering eyes. *Isn't this what I always wanted? Someone whose passion knows no bounds? Someone who holds me so tight I can't breathe, kisses me so hard my teeth break, my bones ache.* I look around. Others are following me. I am a Pagan alone in a Muslim culture, skin pure white, blue eyes, red hair. I hear my dear friend calling in my ears, "take it in, take it in." I breathe a heavy sigh and continue up the hill by the wall that surrounds the Medina. I know there are seven gates into this neighborhood. When I come upon the next one I enter, wary of all who look at me. I keep my eyes down, walk straight, no swinging hips. I am a life dancer of grace, elegance, and beauty radiant. Even in my oversize blue djellaba. I enter the Souk and the shop keepers call out to me, "Welcome, come look, we have beautiful things." I walked down these isles just yesterday, a smile on my face, eyes shining. But today I am afraid. I round the next corner and there he is. Standing. Looking at me with the eyes of a tiger. Charged. He speaks. "Aji la hana." Meaning "come here" in Arabic. I do as he bids and find myself inches from his eyes and mouth I have taken less than an hour ago. His energy potion fills me with longing I have never felt before and suddenly I find myself walking, as if in a dream, with him, back to his house. The language barrier strong. The language of passion stronger. When I enter his house, he stands looking at me. "Why you leave?" he says. And thinking of the simplest way to tell him my feelings I say, "you move me," holding my hand to my heart. Without saying a word he moves closer to me. Closer. I can smell his sweet rooty breath, feel his virile pulse pounding on my chest. Closer. I want him. Now. Standing there, looking into those dark eyes that see everything about me. *Take it in.*

The night before we lay together. Wrapped deep. He opened me. An opening of lovemaking I had only dreamt about. It was after a beautiful home cooked Tajine of chicken, peas, onions, carrots, potatoes, olives and lemons. He served tea in the traditional way, pouring it high from the pot for the many bubbles it produces. I sit fascinated by his hands, his voice, the graceful way he eats with his fingers. His hands thick,

strong and brown. His manner peaceful and confident. I sit patiently in my own juices, that have started to flow, so soon, between my legs. I feel his knowing of this by the way he looks at me. Something about him seems to know everything about me. *Ahhh, intuitive intelligence.* He is fully clothed and taking me then and there without touching me makes my passion for eating strong. After dinner he moves beside me. Sitting close he gently and firmly presses his leg next to mine. The silence contemplating its next move. *I shouldn't have come. This will never work.* He turns, looks in my eyes and leans in to kiss me. I turn my head the other way and he moves back. When I look back at him his eyes hold a deep calling for me I cannot resist. I fall in his trance and move, kissing him gently, lightly. My pulse rises and suddenly I find myself pressed against him, writhing in ecstasy. An animal released from its cage. He captures me totally, moving with me in rhythm of heart. He grasps my hair with both his hands and we tumble down on his tribal Berber rug. The power of his manhood at full attention. My womanhood ready for submission. Opening myself to him like lotus open to the sun, "Take me," I say. His hardness against my thigh, I begin to ride it, hard. His hands grope my back, legs, ass. Reaching wetness, I climax from the anticipation. Our passion grows wilder, hesitation disappears. He removes my scarf, blouse, skirt and I lay half naked before him. I move to remove his clothes but he tells me, "No." This is too much to bear. The ache between my legs growing and lower belly calling out, fuck me now! He enjoys watching me long for him. A smile on his face, he reaches out and cups my breasts and, through my bra, gently twists my teats. I begin to moan. Feeling the sensation between my legs I pull him to me and kiss him hard. My hands reaching for his body to come closer, come in me. His slow hand moves to my wetness and my climax explodes again. I lay there beside him, my body jerking from orgasm. My mind gone. He slowly unveils himself of his djellaba of green and gold without taking his eyes off of me. I see his hardness for the first time. He is large and thick, veins bulging. He lifts me on top of him and we begin to move together in rhythm of camels going through the sands of the Sahara. Slow, powerful, graceful. We know each other. I am on top of him and he is giving me permission to do with him what I want. As I move I feel the slow intake of his huge manhood. First just the tip and as I open I find I can take all of him. Down on him I go. My vagina wet with longing, wet with the language of deep love sex. Hours plunging in and out, stop and go, tender rough. He is strong with keeping his juices within until I am satisfied. And then he begins his journey

to zenith and rises, mounting me from behind. As he moves inside me, my orgasm explodes again and again and he whispers that he is coming to me. "Yes, yes", he whispers. We fall exhausted, side by side, holding each other. Our breathing heightened and our energy completely spent.

He asks me to stay the night and in my sexy trance-like state I say yes. We move to his bedroom and he undresses me completely and gives me a soft gown to wear. I slip into bed all the while watching him move about the room. His smooth chocolate skin, his graceful hands and movements catching me between the thighs. *Will I ever want to stop sexing that?* The bulge and lines of his muscles and bone structure penetrating my whole being. He moves in beside me, takes me in his arms and we sleep.

The next morning he wakes me with his hardness and we exhaust ourselves making love. As he lie sleeping, my wide awake bewildered mind begins to spin. My emotions tangled. My doubts playing havoc with my body. I want to run. I want to devour him body and soul. I want to stay. I want to run. *This is crazy crazy. Stop thinking! Take it in!* I impulsively jump up, quietly dress and rush outside the Medina, where the wall holds its boundaries. I begin climbing the narrow path, running like a woman gone insane. My body still quivering from the lovemaking. *Where am I going? What do I feel? Why am I here?* I lean, breathless against the Medina wall. My thoughts only of him, us, this, Morocco, is this real.

And now, with him standing a breath away, so strong, so inviting, so willing...whatever this spell is...I want more. Deeper.

About the Author

Ahu Smith, a North American artist, is known primarily for her multidisciplinary and multidimensional work. She has performed and exhibited internationally as an actress, singer, performance artist, sculptor, poet, and dancer.

Ahu lives in Stockholm, Sweden, where she writes, holds *StoryDance* workshops, raises a teenager and runs her company "Authentic Traveler", taking groups on themed living retreats to Morocco.

Deep Gratitude

Ana Arango for your personal and professional support.
Linda Ghaderi for your inspired mentoring.
Luciana Amado for picking up the pieces.
Tania Gonzalez Ortega for your friendship against all odds.
Urszula Fijalkowska for making the cover possible.
My sons, Lander and Shine. Without your love I would perish.
The Sahara for its velvet magic.
Youness Oulahbib for showing me.